Revive Us Again
A Daughter's Spiritual Journey

Sharon Lundgren

DEDICATION

I dedicate this book to the power of the Holy Spirit, and to its manifestation in the formation and continual revival of the Glory Bound Singers, and revival of Daughters of the King chapters here and throughout the world. As the scripture says, "All of them were filled with the Holy Spirit…" Acts 2:4

REVIEWS

"This story details the providential acts of God in the life of one family wanting to serve Him. I was blessed to be part of it."
Rev. Dr. A.S. Lawrence

"Sharon is truly a "force of nature" when it comes to Daughters of the King. Everything she has had a vision for in DOK has come to pass, with great success. We have been friends for over 30 years, and this book will recount many of our joint efforts to praise God through the gift of music!"
Nancy McCann, Directress, The Glory Bound Singers

"Sharon Lundgren is one of the most remarkable people I have ever met. Her story, both personal and the DOK has many fascinating twists and turns, and best of all, continuing service as National President of the Order. I have been honored to know her and privileged for a time to work beside her."
Rev. Michael Gemignani, Province 7, DOK Chaplain

"Many people talk about faith, but there is a huge difference between talking and living. Sharon has a dynamic faith she lives out daily in the very context of her life. She is a wonderful witness for our Lord and Savior."
Rev. Dr. John M. Himes, OSF, D. Min, rector, Trinity Episcopal Church, Marshall TX

"Sharon Lundgren is one of those people who can sense the hand of God in all her circumstances. And she has the grace to respond to that presence, regardless of the immediate details, with deep gratitude. Her story is full of it."
Rt. Rev. William Frey, DOK National Chaplain, 2003-2006

CONTENTS

REVIVE US AGAIN

We praise Thee, O God!
For the Son of Thy love,
For Jesus Who died,
And is now gone above.

Refrain:
Hallelujah! Thine the glory.
Hallelujah! Amen.
Hallelujah! Thine the glory.
Revive us again.

We praise Thee, O God!
For Thy Spirit of light,
Who hath shown us our Savior,
And scattered our night.

All glory and praise
To the Lamb that was slain,
Who hath borne all our sins,
And hath cleansed every stain.

All glory and praise
To the God of all grace,
Who hast brought us, and sought us,
And guided our ways.

Revive us again;
Fill each heart with Thy love;
May each soul be rekindled
With fire from above.

Lyrics by William P. Mackay, 1863
Copyright: Public Domain

ACKNOWLEDGMENTS

For his encouragement and editing skills, I thank Rev. Dr. A.S. Lawrence. For my prayer partners, Andrea Evans and Ginny Zuppann, I give eternal thanks. For the Glory Bound Singers, my inspiration in spirit and song, I give everlasting thanks.

PREFACE

Why did I choose the title "Revive Us Again?" There are several reasons. I have been a Daughter of the King for half my life. My children do not know me without a DOK cross. When I joined the Order as a young mother, the Order numbered about 7000 worldwide. Over these last 30 years, I have seen the membership grow to over 30,000 – now on every continent and in Jerusalem! To me that is the best example of "revival" that I can think of. As I write my personal and spiritual journey, you will see how the Lord has woven the Daughter's history into my life. I have personally helped establish five chapters and have helped to revive many more. I am rejoicing in what the Lord has allowed me to participate in as a Daughter. My prayer is that others may be encouraged to pray for "REVIVAL" in their families, their churches, and their communities. My prayer is that they too can rejoice in the Lord's blessings.

1 THE EARLY YEARS

Jesus said, "Let the little children come to me." Luke 18:16

In my early childhood we lived in a small rice-farming community in Southeast Texas, with a population of about 300. I was the oldest daughter; my sister, Deborah, 3 years younger; my brother, Gary, 3 years younger than she. The only two churches in the town were the Baptist Church and the Catholic Church.

From the time I can remember anything, I can remember playing "church." The children in the neighborhood would know what I was planning for our playtime by looking into our garage to see how I had set up the chairs. Theater style would mean "church," and in rows would mean "school." Those were my two favorite play scenes.

My mother, Elwanda Burgess, was a Baptist, and took us to church every Sunday. I loved the Sunday School. The teachers were so kind and the stories of Jesus enthralled me from the beginning. When the boy gave his lunch of loaves and fishes to Jesus, who made that small offering into a miracle, I was fascinated. I could have heard that story over and over --and often I did. My father, J.W. Burgess, was not a Baptist. He had been raised by his Church of Christ mother, and he decided not to join a church as a child. He came to faith in his forties, and lived a very fine life. My mother introduced my father to Bible Study Fellowship, where she had been a teaching leader. My Father loved it, and participated for 12 years after he turned 70 years old.

My mother encouraged us to look at books even before we could read. When I was six she gave us a set of Childcraft Books, and with it came a Children's Study Bible. She gave it to me, and I have kept it all these years. I loved to look at the color pictures of Abraham, Moses, Jesus and Mary — and all the others. Those words and pictures came to life for me in a very

1

real way.

When I was nine years old I came to faith and baptism formally, but I felt that I had known Jesus from the time of my earliest memories. I still remember the night of my baptism, the hymns that were played, and even the dress I wore. It was a very important event for me. When I stepped into the baptismal water, I began to shake. The pastor, thinking I was frightened reassured me that all was well. But I was not afraid; I was curious. Later in life I learned that this shaking can be a manifestation of the Holy Spirit. That is what I claim it to be.

You will learn of my Catholic experience in the next chapter, but I am grateful to have had a special friend in the third grade that took me to her Catholic church and gave me a wonderful glimpse into what my future would hold for me – I just did not know it at the time.

My teen years had some difficulties like everyone else, and my family moved to a larger town. We also started attending a Methodist church. It was more formal, and my father was the choir director. He was a trained band, orchestra, and choral director. Those years in high school gave me an introduction to liturgical worship, and I was drawn to it. But I will have to say, in my heart, I was still a Baptist girl.

Like many young adults of my generation, college gave me lots of opportunities to forget about my spiritual life. I fell away from church for several years, and that was dangerous for me. However, I always felt the Lord was near, protecting me from harm – and HE was!

After college I moved to the big city of Houston. Millions of people and cars everywhere! I worked as secretary to one of the managers at the Houston Post newspaper. That is where I met my husband, Rich. Houston is also the city where God led me into new spiritual experiences that transformed my life completely.

Me at about 8 years old

From left to right: My mother, my sister, Deborah, me, my brother, Gary, and my dad

2 BACKSLIDING BAPTIST

"Return to me and I will return to you, says the Lord." Malachi 3:7

During the fall of 1975 I was planning my wedding to be held sometime in the spring of 1976. My husband-to-be, Rich Lundgren, was a writer/editor for the Houston Post newspaper. He and I were very much in love, and planning our life together when God changed our plans suddenly.

In September I went for my yearly checkup, and the doctor found a problem that needed attention. I was shocked to find out that I might have a cancerous tumor on my ovary. I had not had any symptoms but the doctor had discovered it during my examination. So wedding plans were put on hold, and plans for surgery were made.

My spiritual life had been spent in the Baptist church. Rich had been involved in the Methodist church. We were not attending any church regularly at the time. In Baptist's terms, we were BACKSLIDERS.

I knew that I had to go to church before my surgery, and the Lord impressed upon me that I should also take Holy Communion. That is a very unusual thought for a Baptist, but that is what I knew I must do. I asked Rich if he knew of any church close by where I could take Holy Communion. I did not care what denomination it was. He said he had seen a new church building recently that had a sign out front that said, "Holy Communion Every Sunday – 11:00AM." Rich could not remember the name of the church or the denomination. I laughed and said it sounded just right for us. We made plans to attend.

That Sunday morning changed my life forever. When we drove into the parking lot, the church name was visible: Episcopal Church of the Epiphany. As we entered the sanctuary, I was spellbound by what I saw and felt. The atmosphere was so powerful: the beauty of the new building, walls in soft tones, candles lit, music softly preparing hearts to worship, and then the processional with choir and full regalia. It was as though I had stepped back into my childhood.

You remember that I told you about my childhood Catholic friend and the two churches, Baptist and Roman Catholic, in our town?

My best friend, Mary Neu, invited me to spend the night with her on a Saturday. I realized that I would be going to church with Mary the next morning, and she went to the Catholic Church. I had never been to any Catholic Church, and I was a little frightened because I knew it was different from my church. But a grand surprise awaited me.

When we entered the sanctuary the next morning at Mary's church, I was immediately caught up in the beauty of everything: the flowers, the candles on the altar table, soft paintings on the walls of Jesus and Mary, and the beautiful music before the service even began. Then the priest came forward in his black robe, and he looked strange to me. My pastor only wore a suit. The priest began to preach about Jesus being the Good Shepherd. Then the members went forward and received bread and wine of the Holy Communion. Mary and I just got a blessing from the priest. I liked that feeling. I did not realize until many years later that the Lord was showing me with my childlike faith the beauty of liturgical worship.

I do want to say how grateful I am to have been in the Baptist church as a child. I am grateful to my Mother for taking me there. I was a Sunbeam, a member of Girls Auxiliary, and I loved Sunday School. Above all I love that I was taught the Word of God as a child, and that Word has never left me.

Now back to entering the Episcopal Church of the Epiphany in 1975 for the first time.

The Rev. Joseph DiRaddo began the service with vigor and drama, which later I realized was his style. His sermon especially touched me because along with scripture, he also quoted a prayer I am familiar with - "The Serenity Prayer."

"God, grant me the serenity to accept the things I cannot change, courage to change the things I can, and wisdom to know the difference."

I knew that prayer because several people in my family were members of Alcoholics Anonymous, and that was a prayer used regularly by AA.

After the sermon we were invited to Holy Communion, which is what I was waiting for. Fr. Joe was smiling the entire time he placed the bread into each person's hand. It was so personal and beautiful to me, and I was grateful to have received "the body of Christ."

As we sang the closing hymn, I told Rich that I wanted to sneak out a side door and not speak to anyone – especially that priest. Just as I said that, Fr. Joe stopped as he walked down the aisle, looked at me and said,

"Please do not leave without talking to me." He smiled that big, Italian smile, and I knew I was trapped.

As we shook hand with Fr. Joe at the door, he asked why we were there. I am the talkative one, but I could not say a word. Rich is very quiet, but he started telling Fr. Joe that I needed surgery, etc. I was horrified. Fr. Joe looked at me and asked if I had a priest. I laughed and told him I was a backsliding Baptist. He laughed and said, "Oh good, then you do not have a priest."

He asked me when the surgery was to take place, what hospital, and the time. I told him and he said he would be there before I went into surgery. I thanked him, and we left the church. However, I did not believe he would really come to the hospital. I just thought he was being kind.

On the morning of the surgery, my mother and Rich were there with me. As time came near for them to take me to surgery, Rich said he was surprised that Fr. Joe had not come to see me. I told him I was not surprised. Fr. Joe had a big church, lots of people to take care of, and so forth. The nurses came in and put me on a gurney. All of a sudden the door opened, and there was Fr. Joe – smiling and relieved that he had not missed me.

Fr. Joe gathered the nurses, my mother and Rich around the gurney and prayed for me to be healed, in Jesus's name. I felt this power surge through me, a warm sensation permeated by body. I kept looking into Fr. Joe's eyes. He then said to me, "No matter the outcome of this surgery, Jesus is with you." Then I was taken away. My mother had no idea who this person named Fr. Joe was, but he then took her to coffee and charmed her within minutes. Rich was so relieved.

The next 5 days were a blur for me, but then I got the good news: no cancer, however, they did remove an ovary and a fallopian tube. Chances of a later pregnancy were not so good, but we were grateful for the outcome.

When I called Fr. Joe to tell him the news, he told me that at Church of the Epiphany they have a healing service every Thursday night. He said that everyone who has been healed should be there, so he hoped to see us when I had recovered from the surgery. That Sunday afternoon I received a beautiful flower arrangement from the church – the altar flowers. Rich and I were astounded by the gesture, and would never forget it.

I could say, "The rest is history."

We started attending the healing services on Thursday nights, and Sunday services as well. Five months later, March 19 – St. Joseph's Day – we were married at that altar.

When people in my family asked me later why I became an Episcopalian, I would say, "That is where Jesus healed me.....in the Episcopal Church."

The rest of the story is that we were able to have children: Adam Wayne in 1977, Andrew Joseph in 1980. As the angel Gabriel said to the Virgin Mary, "With God all things are possible." Luke 1:37

Our wedding with Fr. Joe DiRaddo

Together

3 BECOMING A DAUGHTER OF THE KING

"I have called you by name; you are mine." Isaiah 43:1

During 1978 my husband and I were getting more involved in our church life at Epiphany in Houston, TX. Our baby son, Adam, was born in November 1977 and that had tied me down to home. But by fall of 1978 I was ready to do more and I was lonely. I needed friends, and I asked the Lord to show me where HE wanted me to use my gifts in the church.

One Sunday morning before worship, I was sitting quietly praying about these things. I looked up and saw the women who were on the Altar Guild preparing the linens and vessels for the communion service. They looked so peaceful and reverent, and I thought that might be a nice group for me to join.

The next morning after breakfast and while the baby was napping, I called the church office. I quickly said that I would like the name and phone number of the lady in charge of the Altar Guild because I wanted to volunteer my services. There were several seconds of silence before the secretary said in a lofty voice, "My dear, you have to be invited to join the Altar Guild. You do not volunteer."

I froze in my seat, and hung up the phone without saying a word. I was in a panic for a full five minutes until I realized that I had not given the woman my name. Thank God for that! No Altar Guild for me.

Several weeks later I was again praying before the service, and the choir was rehearsing. I immediately got excited about the music, and realized that that might be the group I should belong to. I had been in choirs throughout school and college. My father was a band and orchestra and choral director. He was my first music teacher. Yes, I thought that that is what I should do.

When the service ended, I went up to the choir mistress and told her I would like to join her choir. She looked me up and down, and then asked if I had had any training. I told her of my music history, and she smiled. Then she asked what part I sang, and I told her I was a soprano. She smiled again and then said, "Thank you but I do not need any sopranos right now." I just turned and walked away. No choir for me.

My husband was involved with a men's group, and I was feeling very left out. Then suddenly one Friday morning I got a call from a lady I had met at the coffee hour after church. Her name was Jane Taylor. Jane invited me to come the next morning to her ladies group where they pray, study the Bible, and work on whatever service project our priest had asked them to help with. I told her I had the baby, and she said to bring the baby because they had childcare. She never mentioned the name of her ladies group.

The next morning I went to the Parish Hall to meet Jane and the others. There were women of all ages: young mothers with children, working women, and gray-haired retirees. They welcomed me and took the baby to the nursery. We had prayer and Bible study, and it was not until Jane asked them to say their motto that I learned this group is called The Order of the Daughters of the King!®

FOR HIS SAKE

I am but one, but I am one.

I cannot do everything, but

I can do something.

What I can do, I ought to do.

What I ought to do,

By the grace of God,

I will do.

Lord, what will you have me do?

When I heard the words of the motto, I knew God was calling me to be a Daughter of the King. The ladies in that chapter took me in, wrapped me in the love of Jesus, and gave me a place to belong. I had prayed for godly friends, and God answered me with POWER!

4 THE EPIPHANY YEARS, 1975-1988

"Whenever you face trials of any kind, consider it joy, because you know that the testing of your faith produces endurance..." James 1:2

We were members of Epiphany Episcopal Church for 13 years. It was such a blessed time for me in so many ways: confirmation classes, the birth of our children and their baptisms, working in ministry, and Rich's election to vestry several times. The Lord was teaching me, stretching me my in faith, and grounding me deeper in the Word and church history.

Fr. Joseph DiRaddo was a gifted teacher for our Confirmation Class. When I realized the factual history of the Episcopal Church, and its connection to our founding fathers of our nation, I was overjoyed. George Washington is one of my favorite people. When I learned that George and Martha were not only the first President and First Lady of the land, but that they were among the first Episcopalians, I told my husband, "If this church is good enough for George Washington, it is good enough for me!"

However Rich, being a writer, was very focused on words and documents. We actually went through 3 classes before being confirmed. Rich did not like the Prayer of Humble Access: "I am not worthy so much as to gather the crumbs under thy table..." He and Fr. Joe had a terrific discussion about worthiness.

Rich asked Fr. Joe if we couldn't be regular visitors, and not be confirmed. Fr. Joe was horrified, and said, "You cannot be on the vestry unless you are confirmed!" Rich then asked what the vestry was. How funny we were back then, and so innocent of church politics and tradition.

Finally, Rich relented and agreed to be confirmed in the next class. But we got the flu, so had to wait until the next (3rd) class was offered. When we were finally confirmed, Fr. Joe told the congregation he had never had any fail Confirmation Class – but the Lundgrens were on their third try!

Several exciting and fulfilling programs were offered to us, and we participated with enthusiasm: Marriage Encounter, Cursillo, and Family Camp at Camp Allen were high points for us.

Our sons were born 2 ½ years apart. Adam was born in 1977 and Andrew was born in 1980. We loved being parents, and had great fun with our boys. They enjoyed going to Discovery Center, the preschool modeled after the Montessori method. They also loved Sunday School, Summer Camp at Camp Allen, choir, and youth group.

When Adam was 9 years old, he came to me and said he would like to be in the children's choir. The same choir mistress that had rejected me was still on staff. I call her and she agreed to meet Adam. At their meeting she asked Adam if he could sing. He started singing for her immediately, and she knew he really could sing. Then she said to him, "Adam, if you join my choir, you will be the only boy. Only girls are in the choir right now." Adam thought a minute, and then smiled as he said, "Then put me in the middle!" She was trapped, and of course put Adam in the middle. Soon other boys came forward to join, perhaps sometimes to her chagrin, but Adam was happy. His mother was delighted!

Drew loved Discovery Center. He loved all the activities, but his favorite day was called "Mud Day." There was a playground attached to the center with several large sand boxes. On "Mud Day" the children would come dressed in swimsuits and the playground would be filled up with water, making every inch muddy. The boys and girls would play in the mud, making artwork on the fences with colored soaps and foams. They mad mud pies and all kinds of critters out of the mud clay. Then they would all be hosed down and cleaned up for going home time. What fun!

My time during these years was spent in ministry with the Daughters. I grew to know and love each of the women in our chapter, and was honored to serve in several leadership positions.

Rich was elected to Vestry three times. He served as Junior Warden and then our last year at Epiphany, he served as Senior Warden during 1988. Fr. Joe took a call in 1982 to be rector of a large church in San Antonio. Two other rectors served the congregation over the next 6 years.

During the spring of 1988 a great division within the congregation developed. It was a very hard time for us and for many. By June my husband had resigned his position as Senior Warden, and we knew we must leave Church of the Epiphany.

Our last Sunday was a very hard day for me. I hated to leave the Daughters of the King who had loved me and helped me so often. But I knew that the Lord was saying that it was time to move on to a new path in our spiritual journey.

Our God is an awesome God, and I did not realize then that HE had prepared a new church home for us that was "far beyond what we could have asked for or imagined." Ephesians 3:20

We simply had to ask the Lord where HE wanted us to go, and HE would direct our path. He directed us to Church of the Ascension in Houston. The years at Ascension proved to be far more fruitful and joyful than anything we had experienced at Epiphany.

In 2003 after I was elected National President, the Daughters at Epiphany sent me a hand-carved cross made from driftwood as a gift of friendship. That was a blessing to me, and helped to heal my heart over things past. God is good!

Adam's Baptism

Adam, age 8
Drew, age 6

5 THE ASCENSION YEARS – NEW BEGINNINGS

"We know that we have passed from death into life because we have love for one another." 1 John 3:14

The summer of 1988 was hard for us after leaving Epiphany. We visited several Episcopal churches in our area, but none seemed to be what we were looking for. Then we remembered that someone had said we should visit Ascension Church in west Houston. We heard they were doing a lot with small group fellowships, and it sounded interesting.

The Sunday we visited with our two boys, age 8 and 10, was a hot summer day. However, the atmosphere inside the church was lovely. We were impressed with the beautiful stained-glass windows that circled the sanctuary. Each window depicted a Bible story. The raised altar was strikingly simple but dramatic. The acoustics were incredible, and made the choir and organ sound glorious.

During the sermon our son, Adam, whispered to me that this is where he wanted to go to church. He had not commented on the other churches we had visited. Adam said later that he really liked the sermon, and the music.

After services several folks came up to welcome us. They invited us to coffee hour and then to their home fellowship group. We really felt the love of the Lord that day.

The Rev. Dr. A. S. Lawrence was the rector. After we had visited services several weeks, he asked us to come to his office for a visit. He knew of the happenings at Epiphany, and wanted to hear what Rich had to say. At that meeting Rev. Lawrence asked us if we were ready to transfer membership to Ascension, and we said that we were ready. He seemed pleased, and we all agreed to the transfer of membership.

The Christian Education Director, Bernice Ruczko, was so delightful.

She was like every child's grandmother. Our boys loved her. Youth group was a big plus as well, with the Rev. Mark Wright in charge.

We visited the home fellowship of Don and Mary Sears, and felt like we had really come home. We would meet every week, have prayer and Bible study. The friends we made in the fellowship are still some of our dearest friends today.

Over the next several months 6 women from the congregation came to me asking about my Daughter's of the King background. They too were Daughters and wanted to start a chapter at Ascension. They asked me to contact Rev. Al and get permission to form the chapter. I agreed to do that.

I made the appointment with Rev. Al, and put together a folder including all pertinent information about our DOK ministry. When we met in his office, I fully expected him to give me 5 minutes, shake my hand, and tell me he would get back to me soon. However, I was very wrong. He opened the folder and went through it page by page, and began to ask me direct questions. I broke into a cold sweat, as I realized how serious he was about this ministry called Daughters of the King. He wanted to be sure I was serious too!

When Rev. Al was pleased with the information I shared, he agreed to set the date for an orientation of the women. Soon we had 23 women in training. The new chapter included Dawn Lawrence, wife of the rector, and Laurel Wright, wife of the associate rector, Rev. Mark Wright. We were thrilled by their support. The chapter was instituted in 1989.

I agreed to be chapter president, and we began regular monthly meetings. We formed prayer teams, took training, and began to pray for people at each eucharist. We offered special speakers to present Quiet Days for all the women of the congregation. We also began to facilitate Alpha Courses on a regular basis. This chapter grew in power and strength over the years, and produced two National Presidents: Sharon Lundgren and Joan Dalrymple. The chapter also produced the Glory Bound Singers in 1991. Praise God for His faithfulness!

Rich was elected to the vestry several times, and served as Junior Warden. He also joined the Chuck Colson Prison Fellowship ministry, with 3 of his best friends. He worked in that ministry for 4 years.

Adam loves to sing, and joined the children's choir. I joined the Chancel Choir!. Everyone welcomed us. Adam was allowed to sing solos for special events. He sang a solo at his own Confirmation service. Adam also went on his first mission trip at age 14 to Honduras to help build a community center for a village that had no electricity. He had never seen such poverty, and also such generosity of spirit. The villagers were so grateful, that on the last day of the mission, Adam learned that the village had given up its meat rations for the week to make a feast for them to enjoy.

Drew is a writer, poet, and actor. He wrote a story in 4th grade and asked the teacher if he could join the Writer's Club at his school. She told him that club was only for 6th grade students. Drew objected, and brought her his story. After she read the story, she was so impressed that she relented, and allowed Drew to join the club. Drew was so proud that the next Sunday he brought that story to Rev. Al for his approval. Several days later Drew received a letter from Rev. Al praising him for his effort, and for the message in his story.
Drew still has that letter and that story in his portfolio.

When Drew was in 6th grade, his Sunday School class wrote an Easter story of the crucifixion. Drew was the only boy who would agree to be Jesus, because he did not mind taking his clothes off! However, he did not like what they had written for Jesus to say at the Resurrection. So Drew wrote his own lines. Drew came out of the grave shouting, "I'm alive....I'm alive....I'm alive!" The crowd loved it!

Rich and I are so grateful that the Lord led us to Ascension Church while our boys were young enough to receive the teaching and nurturing that they were given there. Because Rev. Dr. A.S. Lawrence is grounded in the Word, our boys received the truth of the scriptures, and they still remark about that today.

I thank God for leading us to Ascension Episcopal Church, and pray blessings on that congregation today and always.

with Rev. Al Lawrence

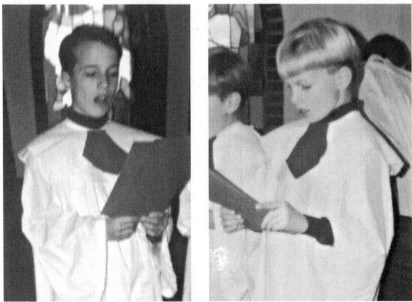

Adam and Drew singing in the choir

6 THE EVANGELISM YEARS

"The gracious hand of my God was upon me." Nehemiah 2:8

The Episcopal Church declared the decade of the 1990s to be the Decade of Evangelism. The Daughters of the King grasped the vision and got to work. The National Episcopal Church declined in membership in that decade, while the Daughters of the King grew steadily. We doubled our worldwide membership in that decade, and are now on every continent.

During 1990 I was contacted by the Diocesan DOK Nominating Committee and asked if I would be willing to serve as the next Vice-President of the Texas Diocesan Board. The call was a surprise to me, and I was excited to get this opportunity. Wanda Sinclair was the Diocesan President when I became her Vice-President. Wanda had been a faithful Daughter for many years, and I was blessed to serve with her.

Wanda asked me to look at "communications" and see how we could reach more Daughters around the diocese. This was before the internet, cell phones, etc. I envisioned a newsletter would be a great help in getting information to our women. Laurel Wright from my chapter was a desktop publisher. Laurel accepted the challenge. She and I created "The Angelus" newsletter in July of 1990. Today "The Angelus" is an online publication. Progress!

Already I had had an exciting start to 1990 when my husband, Rich, asked me to accompany him on a business trip to New York. I had recently purchased our DOK 100 Year History Book, and was reading about Church of the Resurrection in New York where Margaret Franklin started the Order. I told the Lord that I would make a pilgrimage to the church. I was thrilled with the prospect of what I would uncover there.

On February 5, 1990 we arrived by taxi at the church door. I was expecting a beautiful Gothic church, dedicated to the legacy of the

Daughters. What I found was a church in disrepair – red doors faded and cracked, tarnished stained glass windows, and a locked door. When the secretary finally answered the door, she did not look happy to see me. I blurted out that I was from Texas, a Daughter of the King, and I hoped this was the right church. Her reply was, "The church is closed on Mondays, and what is a Daughter of the King?"

I was horrified, and my husband was laughing in the background. The taxi had left, so I asked if we could come inside and call for another. She allowed us in, and then I realized I could at least look inside the sanctuary to see if I recognized anything from the history book.

When I walked inside the church, I was surprised to see the carpet faded and torn, the plaster cracked – a church looking very sad and forgotten. Was this really the church where Margaret Franklin had the vision for the Daughters of the King?

The Lord urged me to go into a pew and pray, to be quiet, and observe what I saw. So I did. I prayed that the Lord would show me something that would confirm the history of our founding, and HE did.

When I got up to leave, I went down a hall parallel to the sanctuary. At the end of the hall was a wall plaque. As I got closer to it I realized it had a DOK cross on it. It was tarnished, but I could read the words clearly:

"To the Glory of God, and in commemoration of the fiftieth anniversary of the founding of the Order of the Daughters of the King®, 1885-1935."

Praise God from whom all blessings flow!

As I touched the plaque, these words rushed through my mind and heart:
"You are the salt of the earth, and the light of the world. A city set on a hill, whose light cannot be hid. Restore this and they will come."

Then my husband said it was time to go to catch our plane to Texas. Off we went, and all the way to Texas I pondered what I had just experienced. How could the Daughters have forgotten our founding church? What could we do to help them? Did they have a chapter now?

On my return to Houston, I wrote a letter to the rector, Rev. James Cupit. He is English, and was delighted to communicate with me. He and I spoke by phone on several occasions, and he knew of the ministry of the Daughters. I asked what we could do for the church. He said they needed funds. Lots of funds. I explained that Daughters do not raise money, but we could pray for monies to come in for the church's restoration. Also, the church had a day school and we could help the school by saving soup labels to redeem for supplies. Andrea Evans of St. John the Divine in Houston took over the coordination of the soup label campaign. Daughters began to pray for funds, and to save soup labels.

In July 1990, I received a call from Fr. Cupit. He was very excited. He told me that the church had just received an endowment of nearly $1,000.000.00.

WOW! I told him we had really been praying, and God had answered our prayers with power!

By Christmas Eve 1990, Church of the Resurrection had new paint, new plaster, new carpet, and new light fixtures! The pictures Fr. Cupit sent were lovely.

Fr. Cupit also sent me a copy of the church's 100 Year History Book. It fascinated me to read about all that was done through this church that was founded in 1861, when Margaret Franklin was only 6 years old

Meeting Margaret Franklin

Between the DOK History Book and the Resurrection History Book, the Lord began to plant a vision in me for telling Margaret Franklin's story of how the Order began. It was not until 1996 when my friend, Ginny Zuppan, urged me to write a monologue in first-person as Margaret, that I began to write this seriously. My first costume was a pink-lace bathrobe, and a pink hat with an ostrich feather. What a hoot. When my friend, Nancy McCann, saw me dressed like that, she chided that we would have to get me into a real costume if anyone else was to meet Margaret Franklin! So we put together much more appropriate attire – no bathrobe.

During 1996-97 I began to write the detailed monologue. It has changed over the years, as I have read and learned more about Margaret's life and the life of the Order. My costumes have also changed, and so have my hats. I love hats so this has been a very fun part of my exploration into the history of the Daughters. "Margaret Franklin" has now introduced herself and told her story to many dioceses and provinces, and to at least 2 national retreats.

The Glory Bound Singers

The year 1991 proved to be a year of vision and creativity for me. On June 8, 1991, I attended a Quiet Day of the life of St. Francis of Assisi. Bernice Ruczko, Christian Education Director, was our speaker. She was working on her master's thesis on the life of St. Francis. Her teaching opened my mind to a wonderful possibility. I did not know that St. Francis, before he was called by God, was a minstrel and actor. God used his gifts mightily when Francis heard the Lord say to him in San Damiano Church, "Francis, restore my church." I was reminded that the year before, at

Resurrection Church, I had heard: "Restore this and they will come."

As Francis began his ministry work with the brothers God gave him, they would often go into the villages singing as they went. The people would come out into the streets to hear the songs, and then Francis and his group would act out the life of Jesus. Many came to faith by this visionary style of teaching.

At the end of the Quiet Day, Bernice challenged us to write a prayer that the Lord would give us. As I sat quietly, this is prayer that I wrote down:

"Thank you, Lord, that through the gift of music, we are Glory Bound."

When the day was over, I bought a book on the meditations of St. Francis, and went home happily repeating the prayer God had given me.

The next day our family set out for a vacation to Destin, Florida. As we drove, I kept repeating the prayer. Then I began to ask the Lord who the "we" might be that are Glory Bound?

Each morning we were in Destin, I would go to the surf at sunrise and pray. The Lord began to show me faces of Daughters who were musical. Thus the vision for the Glory Bound Singers came into full view. Our purpose would be to lead worship for DOK assemblies in the Diocese of Texas, Lord willing.

I pondered over the name Destin – so much like Destiny. It is curious to me that the Lord revealed this to me in Destin, at the sea........living water!

When I got back to Houston, I called each of the women whose faces had come to me. Each one thought about what I suggested and said they would give it a try. Some thought I was a bit nutty, but that is OK......being a fool for Christ is not so bad.

Before we began our rehearsals for the September assembly in Texas, I was able to attend my first Triennal Retreat in July in Phoenix, Arizona. I did not know what to expect, but what I experienced surprised me. The first night we gathered for worship, two older ladies played guitars and led us in song. They were kind and sweet people, but the worship was less than robust. It made me wonder if the Lord might have an even bigger plan for the Glory Bound singers. Little did I know what was to come.

Back from Arizona, I set up rehearsals for the new group. None of the ladies played guitar, so I asked two of the husbands who did play to help us. They agreed. The first song the Lord gave me for us to sing is, "Revive Us Again." We continue to sing that song today - 23 years later!

Nancy McCann is a professional musician. I knew she should be the permanent Directress for the Glory Bound Singers, but she was living in Michigan at that time. However, when I called her to tell her of the vision, she was amazed. Her husband's company had just decided to transfer them back to Houston. "With God all things are possible!"

Our first time to lead worship at a Diocese of Texas Assembly was September 19, 1991. The assembly was held at St. Paul's Episcopal Church in Katy, Texas. Esther Miller, our missionary to Malawi, was our special guest. Ginny Zuppan, then Province 7 V-President, was our keynote speaker. Her topic was from Queen Esther: "Who knows but that you have come to the kingdom for such a time as this." What a great lesson for our new music ministry.

The first worship song we sang was, "Revive Us Again."

At the close of the assembly, the husbands told us that from then on we were on our own. We were so grateful for their help, but we needed to raise up women who played guitar and other instruments. We did that. At any given time we now have guitars, flute, piccolo, piano, organ, and zither. The Glory Bound Singers have now led worship for every Diocese of Texas Assembly since September of 1991. We have also led worship for Province 7 assemblies.

We started in 1991 with 12 voices from 2 churches. Today we are nearly 50 voices from 22 different churches. In 2016 we will celebrate our silver anniversary, Lord willing.

Jesus said in John 15:16, "I chose you; you did not choose me. I chose you to bear fruit. Fruit that will last."

Our music has now traveled around the world--from Africa to South America, from Europe to Jerusalem our music is praising God!

To me the most incredible testimony to the call on our music ministry is that we have now led worship at each of these National Triennial Retreats:

Church of the Resurrection, New York in 1997; Denver Triennial 2000; Minneapolis Triennial 2003; Orlando Triennial 2006; Anaheim Triennial 2009; and Indianapolis Triennial 2012. We are currently rehearsing for the Salt Lake City Triennial in 2015. We thank God for these marvelous opportunities to "sing unto the Lord."

Highlights of Leadership

- ❖ 1990 – Elected as Vice President of the Diocese of Texas
- ❖ 1994 – Elected President of the Diocese of Texas
- ❖ 1996– Appointed as V- President of Province 7,serving out a term
- ❖ 1997 – Elected as Province 7 President, serving 1997-2000

During my tenure as Vice President of the Diocese of Texas, my job was communications. This was before the internet, and we did not have a regular newsletter. I was able to create "The Angelus" newsletter with the help of DOK, Laurel Wright, who is also a writer and desktop publisher. Today "The Angelus" is an online publication – progress in the new century.

As President of the Diocese of Texas, I chose as my theme "The Great Commission." I encouraged our women to "make disciples", as Jesus requested in Matthew 28. It was during this time that the Diocese of Texas grew to be the largest membership of any diocese in the United States. We still today have the largest membership. God is good.

Nehemiah

During Advent 1994 the Lord impressed upon me to study the book of Nehemiah. When I prayed I thought the Lord would direct me to a gospel, but HE sent me to Nehemiah. Out of Nehemiah came a marvelous vision regarding the Daughters.

Nehemiah was a Jew living in Persia as slave to the king, 450 years before Jesus was born. The Lord had placed upon Nehemiah's heart a desire to return to Jerusalem. He had learned that the walls of the city were broken down, and the Jews were left unprotected. The Persian King favored Nehemiah and allowed him to return to Jerusalem. When Nehemiah saw the broken down walls, he knew he was to rebuild the walls for his people. He recruited families to do this work. He was so successful that within 52 days they had restored the walls around Jerusalem.

Then Ezra the scribe came out to the people, and opened the Word of God to them. Many had never heard it. When they heard the Word, they repented of their sins and asked God to be their God Almighty. Nehemiah was able to save the Jews physically and spiritually through re-building the walls.

I asked the Lord what this might mean for Daughters. The vision the Lord gave me was this: Daughters of the King should "build a wall of Prayer" around their homes, families, the nation, and the world, that the Ezra's can come forth and proclaim the Word to them. I especially felt that Daughters should "build a Wall of Prayer" around Jerusalem. Seventeen years later, the Lord allowed us to do just that.

In 1995 the Daughters of the Diocese of Texas celebrated our centennial. We began in Waco, Texas in 1895 at St. Paul's Episcopal Church. We went back to that church in 1995 to mark our celebration. Mrs. Mattie Hayes Howe was the founding Daughter of Texas. She had no children. The Daughters of the King and the Sunday School were her beloved ministries. At her death in 1901, the Daughters of St. Paul's ordered a stained glass window, 8 feet by 10 feet, to be made in her honor. It depicted Jesus as "The Good Shepherd," holding a lamb. The scripture was, "Feed my Lambs."

Our Spring Assembly in 1996 was held at St. Matthew's in Austin, TX. I invited our National President, Laurie Ann Herman, to be our luncheon speaker. A very special guest, Helen Grace Wangusa, of Uganda, was our keynote speaker. Helen was a Daughter of the King, and poet laureate of her country. She had asked if we might find 3 wedding dresses that she would take back to Uganda for the women to borrow for their weddings. To her surprise the Daughters responded miraculously by providing 142 wedding gowns, which we hung across the parish hall walls covering every inch of wall space. It was glorious. Helen wept when she saw the generosity of the women of Texas.

President Laurie Ann Herman was inspired by our Texas Assembly, and the Glory Bound Singers. After she returned home, she called me and asked if we could bring the Glory Bound Singers to New York the next summer to lead worship at Church of the Resurrection for the closing service of the Triennial of 1997. I was surprised and delighted to get that invitation, as was our Directress, Nancy McCann, and our members. How good of God to invite us to the church where our Order was founded!

When summer of 1997 arrived, we were able to bring 28 singers to New York for that service. What a glorious day it was for us and for our DOK sisters – all 331 that attended that day. The rector had never seen his church filled until the Daughters of the King filled it. The church only seats 250, so folding chairs had to be brought in. Also, no air conditioning, so fans were in order. But no matter the heat or the crowd, we were all joyful!

At the end of the service we received an invitation to go to Denver in 2000 to lead the worship for Triennial 2000. The theme they had chosen was "Revive Us Again." Of course we could not refuse.

Many other events occurred during the 1990s, but the ones I have shared are the most significant ones to me personally. I am grateful for all the DOK around the world who dedicated themselves to introducing others to Jesus during this decade.

25

Margaret Franklin

Me dressed as Margaret Franklin

The Glory Bound Singers Banner

The GBS together!

Me with Nancy McCann – 2005

First time in the recording studio – Sharon, Rock, and Nancy - 1996

Me, Rock Romano, and Nancy recording again - 2013

Joy Dyer, Banner Maker for the GBS

7 ST. MICHAEL AND ALL ANGELS

"For everything there is a season...." Ecclesiastes 3:1

There was a short time for our family in Longview during the 1990s. We moved to East Texas because Rich had been offered a position as Business Editor at the Longview News Journal, and Longview is where my parents lived. The boys were in middle school and high school.

I had served on the Diocese of Texas DOK Board with Cynthia Brust, now The Rev. Cynthia Brust. Her husband, The Rev. Ellis Brust, was rector of Saint Michael and All Angels Episcopal Church in Longview. We moved our membership to SMAA.

Drew was the right age for Confirmation, and he became an acolyte during this time. He enjoyed his acolyte duties, until one certain Sunday. This was the first Sunday that the Altar Guild had placed their new silk floral arrangement on the altar behind the candles. The silk arrangement was beautiful and was very expensive. All was well until time for the recessional. When Drew reached up to snuff out the candles, he accidentally flipped the gorgeous floral arrangement into the choir – much to their surprise. The choir kept singing as they had caught the flowers before they hit the floor. The Altar Guild ladies shrieked in disbelief! Drew froze in his shoes, and Rev. Ellis laughingly handed Drew the cross to march us out of the church, as the congregation smiled and laughed also.

Drew also enjoyed Youth Group. He was a strong member, and always ready to help. Two of his friends were in the group also. The Lord protected Drew when his two friends decided to go to Houston for a retreat, and they invited Drew to go with them. We did not allow him to go because of school activities that were already scheduled. That proved to be a fateful decision. The two young men were killed instantly in a car wreck outside of Houston. Drew helped the youth group come to terms with this untimely death, and Drew showed real maturity during this time. It also proved to show the best of the Rev. Brust's pastoral care, as he ministered to the youth group and the families of the young men.

Drew is like his father, and is definitely a writer. Drew is also an artist. The Christmas he was 13 he made me a woodcut angel that I fell in love with. That angel became the focal point for my banner when I was Diocese of Texas President, and again as Province 7 President. The angel is in flight, with a trumpet, issuing a call to come to the Lord!

Adam decided during his sophomore year in high school that he preferred a more formal type of liturgical worship. Adam on his own transferred his membership to Trinity Episcopal Church near downtown. He really enjoyed singing in the traditional choir, and was able to begin his work in the Longview Opera Repertory Company by this association. Adam also won the lead role in his high school musical, "How to Succeed in Business without Really Trying." It was great fun.

Rich was a lay reader, and elected to Vestry. I helped organize a new chapter of the Daughters of the King. We committed to forming prayer teams to pray with folks after each Eucharist. We also provided speakers for Quiet Days, and hosted a Diocesan Assembly in our second year of formation. I am delighted to say that that DOK chapter is still very vigorous and strong in the parish today.

I have always remembered that Ellis Brust said to me one time, "Rich is a writer, but you will be too someday." I had no idea why he said that, but I count it as prophetic.

In our fourth year in Longview, Rich received an offer to take a very fine position with a Houston firm as a senior technical writer. Our boys were thrilled that we were moving back to Houston. They really are city boys, even though they enjoyed some interesting times in East Texas.

The Rev. Ellis Brust and his wife, Cynthia Brust, in later years left Longview to take another call. Now they are both part of the Anglican Mission in America. Cynthia felt the call to the priesthood and was ordained in the Anglican church several years ago. They felt the call to AMIA due to theological considerations. May God bless them and their ministry.

When we moved back to Houston in June of 1997, we returned to Ascension Church, which had always been our home parish in our hearts.

The whole family!

8 2000 – THE NEW CENTURY

"Behold, I make all things new." Revelation 21:5

As the new century began, I was serving my last year as Province 7 President, which meant that I had served on National Council for almost three years. I loved meeting the Daughters across Province 7. Many wonderful experiences are in my heart and mind, especially being able to assemble the Diocese of Northwest Texas.

However, to me the premier accomplishment of the National Council in 2000 was the purchase of the Margaret J. Franklin Center in Woodstock, Georgia.

Laurie Ann Herman had asked Bishop Roger White to serve as National Chaplain during her tenure. Fortunately he was able to serve during Sue Schlanbush's tenure as well. Not only was Bishop White a fine Christian leader, he was also a visionary. Bishop White helped our council see the possibilities of owning our own facility for the Order. For over a hundred years we had paid rent. Also, for nearly a hundred years we had been saving the Endowment Fund.

Bishop White was able to show our council how we could trade one asset for another, and pay for our new national center. At that time we had approximately $350,000 in our Endowment Fund. The site we chose would cost approximately $300,000. We prayed and discussed this option fully for several months. Finally we did purchase the property(in a suburb of Atlanta, GA), and we paid cash for it. The Order of the Daughters of the King® hold deed to our own national center. We are independent. Praise God!

Some Daughters were concerned that we had depleted our Endowment Fund. However, the Lord showed us that when we make right choices In His Name, He blesses it. By 2010 the Endowment Fund had increased to nearly $1,000,000 – more than 3 times what it had taken us 95 years to save. God is good!

Today the Margaret J. Franklin Center hosts administrative offices, a chapel, meeting space, and expansive space for our archives. I encourage Daughters to visit the center whenever they can. Thank our office staff for their hard work, and Praise God for all His Blessings!

We dedicated the Margaret J. Franklin Center in October 2000. As we processed into each room of the center, we sang "Hail The Festival Day!" Bishop White blessed each part of the center, and our new National President, Joan Millard prayed for Daughters across the world to give thanks for all God's mercy to us.

National Triennial Retreat, Denver – 2000

Before we got to the October dedication, we did have the Denver Triennial in July 2000.

The Denver Triennial was such fun for the Glory Bound Singers. We worked hard the year before to get ready to lead worship for each service. When we arrived in Denver the hotel was filled with Green Party people and Harley Davidson bikers. They were ending their conventions, as we began our Triennial.

At the check-in desk, a very friendly fellow in biker clothes and tattoos told me he really liked my DOK cross. I told him I was a Daughter of the King. He looked amazed and asked me, "Did you get that cross at Graceland?"

For a minute I was shocked, and then I said smiling, "Not that king – and pointed up to heaven – that King!" We both laughed and waved bye as he went on his way.

The theme for the Triennial was chosen by the National Council: Revive Us Again!

Of course that thrilled the Glory Bound Singers, as we had been singing that hymn for years, since our founding. That hymn also proved to be prophetic, as the election of the new National President showed us all. Joan Millard of Kentucky was elected National President for the new term. Joan felt the Lord was calling her to have the Daughters focus with renewed energy and determination on Prayer, Service and Evangelism. It was a refreshing turning point for many of us within the Order.

Gratefully I was also elected to the National Council. Several council members asked me to stand for 1st Vice-President of the Executive Board. I prayed over that request, and decided to stand. God granted me that position, and I knew quickly what the Lord was calling me to work on. God was impressing upon me to work as Triennial Chair for the 2003 event in Minneapolis. I was envisioning a theme for this Triennial - "Living

Water."

In 2001 I had read for the first time Richard Foster's book, "Streams of Living Water." I immediately knew that this was a book that all Daughters could embrace. The scripture in John 7:38 spoke to me, "Out of your believing heart shall flow streams of living water."

The book traced our Christian history by using the metaphor of streams to show us how to embrace one another's gifts. Here are the streams: Contemplative Stream (Prayer-filled Life); Evangelical Stream (Word-Centered Life); Charismatic Stream (Spirit-filled Life); Holiness Stream (Virtuous Life); Sacramental Stream; Social Justice Stream (Compassionate Life).

The National Council approved my appointment as Triennial Chair, and they agreed upon the theme that I had chosen - "Streams of Living Water."

I contacted Richard Foster's office in Colorado to see if he might be in Texas within a few months. As God would provide, Mr. Foster would be in San Antonio in 2 weeks from our phone call. I set my plan to go to San Antonio, and called my dear friend and prayer partner, Nancy McCann, and asked her to meet me there. She agreed, laughing at my belief in the "powers of persuasion!"

When we arrived at the San Antonio conference, I had brought a folder with all the necessary information about our Triennial Retreat. I also had a formal invitation to Mr. Foster to be our keynote speaker, teaching from his book "Streams of Living Water."

Standing at the book table was a very tall young man, whom I guessed to be on the Foster team. We introduced ourselves to him, and I began to tell him about why I had come to the conference. Here are the words I said:

"My name is Sharon Lundgren. I am a Daughter of the King, and I am on a mission from God."

He laughed and said his name was Lyle Smith-Graybeal, and he wanted to know what my mission was. I quickly told him the purpose of our visit. He seemed very intent on my words, and then told me to get in the line at the break where people have Mr. Foster sign his books. Lyle told me to tell Richard exactly what I had told him. So I did. Nancy stood behind me praying with all her might.

When Richard Foster heard my introduction, he laughed, and said, "I do not know what a Daughter of the King is, but I believe you."

Then I quickly told him of our invitation, and handed him the folder with all the specifics. He smiled and said that he would take this seriously and get back to me within two weeks.

Nancy and I practically danced back to our seats. We had done our part, and now the rest was up to God!

I waited two weeks, and called Richard's office. When the secretary answered the phone, I said, "Hello, I am Sharon Lundgren, a Daughter of the King....."

She interrupted and said, "And you are on a mission from God!" Then she and I laughed and she said that she had good news for me. Richard Foster had agreed to be our keynote speaker for Triennial 2003, in Minneapolis MN. How appropriate our theme turned out to be. Minnesota's slogan is "Land of 10,000 Lakes." Living Water!

Fast forward to the Triennial in 2003. We had nearly 650 women at that retreat – a record. Richard brought a team to help him with the teachings: Felicia Smith-Graybeal, Episcopal priest and Emily Griffin, Roman Catholic author. The three of them were delightful each day as they refreshed us with the knowledge of how God uses our different gifts to equip us for ministry.

Surprises awaited me at the close of this Triennial. I was elected to my third term on National Council. The greatest surprise is that I was also elected to serve as National President of the Order of the Daughters of the King®.

The next three years would prove to be physically and emotionally hard, spiritually uplifting, and would draw me closer to our Lord than ever before. I learned many lessons over and over again, especially "With God all things are possible."

9 PRESIDENTIAL MEMORIES

"Trust in the Lord with all your heart, and do not rely on your own understanding. In all your ways acknowledge HIM and HE will direct your path." Proverbs 3:5-6

The Minneapolis Triennial in 2003 was such joy for me. Just having Richard Foster and his team, along with the Glory Bound Singers was truly heaven's gift to me. I enjoyed all aspects of the Triennial as Triennial Chair. Then came the election of the new council and new executive board officers.

When President Joan Millard came over to me in the closed session, wrapped her arms around me, and announced that I was the newly elected National President, I cried. So did others. My tears were tears of gratitude and shock. I wasn't sure what the others' tears were about, but then we all started to laugh and cheer. That was such a marvelous experience for me personally.

To put on Margaret Franklin's original pin, knowing that I should wear it each day pledging to Pray, Serve and Evangelize just as she had done, was a privilege and overwhelming also. Joan Millard told me that there is an anointing for each woman who wears that pin, and I did believe her as we took our vows in the closing service. I knew I had to rely on the Lord for direction each day, so I asked for wisdom and focus to always do just that.

Joan Millard invited me to stay on after the closing service so she and I could handle the transition more easily. That was a wonderful three days for me, as Joan gave me such good insight into what the future might hold for me. She also prayed with me about choosing a National Chaplain for my tenure. When I looked through my pocket phone directory, the only bishop's name and number I had was Bishop Bill Frey of Boerne, Texas. I took that as a sign from God. Bill and Barbara Frey were special people to the DOK, and Barbara, being a Daughter herself, was delighted when I made the call to invite Bishop Frey to be our new National Chaplain.

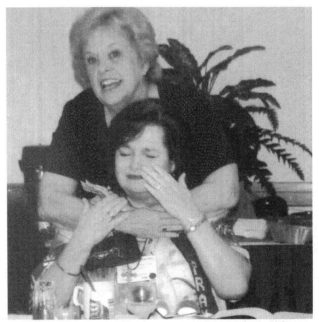

Learning that I had been named National President

When Bishop Frey heard me say that I had been elected as the new DOK National President, he laughed out loud and asked, "How did that happen?" I laughed and said that I really couldn't say, and then he said, "It must be the Lord!" I loved that remark.

Bishop Frey asked some specific questions about the tenure and timing of meetings, etc. Then he said he would take a few days to pray and consider this, and get back to me. Two days later he called and accepted the position. We were all thrilled with his decision.

Bishop Frey always counseled me and our council wisely. When we would get off on a "rabbit trail," he would smile and say, "Ladies let us always keep the "main thing" the MAIN THING. His meaning was clear to us. He was challenging us to see if what we were trying to decide was in the best interest of the Order, was what scripture directed us to do, and was a decision that would further the spread of Christ's kingdom.

Barbara Frey came with the bishop, and she was such a comfort to us all. Her compassion, joy, and love for the Lord always encouraged us in our work. Her teachings on "forgiveness" are well-known and timeless. As I am writing this, Barbara has just entered eternity, and we are all praying for Bishop Frey and their family and friends to be comforted. She will be dearly missed by all.

Next I needed to choose an Advisor for my term, a role which is usually filled by a past National President. Immediately the name of Laurie Ann Herman came to me as she had not served in this position previously, and I already had such a close relationship with her. When I called her, she was delighted and accepted the position. Her love and compassion for all the council members was evident each time we met. When she died in 2012, I was very anguished and still miss her greatly.

My theme for my term came to me in an unusual way. At the end of the Triennial, the Altar Guild ladies asked me to come to the chapel and see what they had discovered. I immediately went into the chapel, and saw a watermark left in the middle of the altar cloth that was the outline of a fish. Immediately the scripture came to me: "Come, follow me, and be fishers of men." Matthew 4:19 Another translation says, "Follow me, and I will make you fish for people!" I like that one too. My husband wears a t-shirt that has written on it:

Fishers of Men,
We Catch 'EM, GOD CLEANS 'EM.

I also love to say that Jesus said, "Come, follow me, and be....." just be.

My theme: Fishers of Men

When I arrived back in Houston, we had a Glory Bound Singer get together to share memories and rejoice that one of our own had been elected National President. Awesome!

I learned within 2 weeks of coming home that life can change in an instant. My husband, Rich, lost his job. I was not working at that time, so we had to pray and decide what the Lord wanted us to do. Rich had been thinking of leaving Houston, and so we explored several possibilities. One was to move outside of Austin to Down Home Ranch, which was a residential facility for young people with disabilities. Judy Horton, co-owner of the ranch with husband Jerry, was a Daughter of the King. Rich would be an employee and I would be a volunteer.

On January 15, 2004 Rich suffered a disabling stroke, and that changed our plans. Suddenly Rich needed a place to heal and I needed to work. I became a Resident Assistant or house mother at Down Home Ranch, and Rich lived with me in the Barnabas House. I had three young men to care for, and Rich. The Lord was directing my path in a very different direction than I had envisioned.

I prayed and asked the Lord if I should resign my position as National President. But Bishop Frey and the Executive Board said that I should not resign. They would help me, and the board would travel for me when I could not travel. It was a gracious, kind, and heartfelt gesture which I will always be grateful for.

At the ranch I was able to "fish for people" in many ways. We had five young ladies who decided they would like to be Daughters of the King. We decided that they should actually be Jr. Daughters, as all of them had disabilities that would prohibit them from going through the senior training with ease. It took them a year to go through the Jr. DOK training, and they were terrific. Their prayer life is incredible. They chose the name of their chapter to be "Little Daughters of the Good Shepherd." They learned the 23rd Psalm by heart; even those who could not read could say the Psalm. At their installation each one proudly received her pin with jubilation. All of us shared tears of joy. This is the first Jr. DOK chapter for young ladies with disabilities, and I am grateful to have been a part of its formation.

My husband and I lived at the ranch until May of 2006. We are grateful for the time we spent with those who some say are "less fortunate." Those young men and women taught us humility and gratitude, and how to find joy in each day.

I was blessed to bring the Executive Board to the ranch for a meeting in spring of 2005. It was wonderful to see our ranchers meet and greet the board members, including Bishop and Barbara Frey, and Laurie Ann and Ron Herman. It was a meeting none of us will ever forget!

Little Daughters of the Good Shepherd – Down Home Ranch

Boys at Barnabus House with Andrew

Theology vs. Politics; Council Meetings

There is lots of work to do at the national level. My Executive Board worked hard to complete the tasks before them to get ready for the first council meeting in November of 2003. Some of my sisters on council have called me "The Maverick." It could be that I often think "outside the box."

The year of 2003 caused some stress within the National Episcopal Church with the election of Bishop Eugene Robinson. Many Daughters of the King were making decisions about whether or not to stay within ECUSA. My council had to tackle the question:

"If a Daughter of the King leaves ECUSA, is she still a Daughter?"
There were mixed feelings on my council as to the answer to that question. Some said that if a woman leaves ECUSA, then she is not a Daughter and should return her cross. Others said that if she goes to the Roman Catholic Church, she surely is still a Daughter since we have had RC DOK since 1986. Others said that if a woman goes to an Anglican Church, she surely is a Daughter because we have had Anglican Daughters since 1892 (first in Canada, then England, now across Africa and South America, Europe, and Jerusalem). After much prayer and discussion, I shared with my council that I thought any woman who had taken our vows and was paying our dues was still a Daughter. We take our vows to the Lord, not to a denomination. But we are grateful for our Episcopal founding and our covering as an Episcopal order. No matter what future decisions might be, I did not feel we should ask for anyone's cross to be returned. My council agreed with that. If any woman felt called to leave ECUSA because of theological reasons, we asked our sisters to pray for her. If any woman felt it was her duty to make others stay in ECUSA for political reasons, we asked our sisters to pray for her also.

Margaret Franklin and our first sisters were not interested in making Episcopalians out of others; they were interested in introducing them to the living God, and his name is Jesus, the Christ. Margaret Franklin thought that if others found a relationship with Jesus in our Episcopal churches, they would naturally want to join us. I feel that way too, even today.

At one of our Triennial meetings, a Daughter came up to me and whispered in my ear, "I am an Anglican Daughter." I have her a big hug and a smile and said, "Let me tell you something very important: Jesus is not an Episcopalian! - He is God Almighty and we are all HIS Daughters."

The next issue regarding Roman Catholic and Anglican Daughters came as a surprise to me. We received letters from RC DOK asking why they could not be delegates to Triennial events, since they had been paying dues like everyone else. Up until that time only Episcopal DOK were allowed to be delegates. Then we received letters from Anglican DOK who had formed new chapters, and they also asked to be delegates to Triennial events. They also were dues paying members. These numbers were very small and could not actually have changed any elections, but the principle was very important. Remember, "no taxation without representation." Our very nation was founded on that principle.

Bishop Frey directed the council to take 24 hours to pray and discuss these issues before we would make a final decision. At the end of that next day, we unanimously voted to allow all members to be equal, with seat and voice at Triennial events. That would not be the end of the discussion. We printed our decision in the Royal Cross and reported that this would be voted on by the delegates at the next Triennial Business Meeting.

Companions on the Way

It was during 2005 that the Lord began to show me a vision to allow women who are not from the episcopate to form Daughter's chapters in their own denomination using our model. I kept hearing the phrase, "They would be our "Companions on the Way." They would be our sisters in purpose and pledge.

I presented this vision to the National Council, and they approved of the idea with enthusiasm. We published this vision in the Royal Cross, and got many encouraging responses. No one complained to me. We made it clear that they could use the name: Daughters of the King. They could not be called The Order of the Daughters of the King®. They would design their own badge. One Lutheran church asked me to help them with this vision. They chose a Greek cross and inscribed the words "For Jesus's Sake" on the crossbar. They also took vows to Pray, Serve and Evangelize. They were under the authority of their Lutheran pastor, and totally independent. What a blessing!

Today this vision is still small, but scripture says not to despise the day of small beginnings. So we pray for all those who might join us one day as "Companions on the Way."

Jerusalem

In 2005 I received the invitation I had been hoping for since 1993. I received an invitation to go to Jerusalem, to Christ Church, and introduce our ministry to the women there. My dear friend and DOK, Martha Macdonald of San Antonio had taken a packet to Christ Church in 2004 with information about our Order. She told the rector, Rev. Tony Higdon, that I would be willing to come and meet with him and speak to the women. That is how the invitation came to me. However, Bishop Frey was the one who first told me about Christ Church. As soon as he became our National Chaplain, I shared with him my hope to form a DOK chapter in Jerusalem. He told me that the church that would more likely embrace our message would be Christ Church. Bishop Frey was right!

Holy Week 2005 was spent in Israel. How marvelous for me to land in Tel Aviv on Palm Sunday. The drive from the airport took us onto the Plain of Sharon. That delighted me – to see the land I was named after. The next week was spent seeing all the sights that are so precious to us as believers. The Sea of Galilee was as lovely as I had hoped it would be. Mount Carmel where Elijah challenged the prophets of Baal, and God came in power, was an amazing site. Then we came to the River Jordan. You know my story about that, which still makes me smile. "One Lord, one Faith, one Baptism."

On Good Friday we entered Jerusalem. It still gives me chills to remember entering the city with the song "Jerusalem" on the CD praising God. We walked the way of the cross, and on Saturday went to the holiest of sites in the old city. On Easter morning at sunrise, we were gathered with 1500 pilgrims from around the world at the Garden Tomb. It was glorious. Sunday evening we were at Christ Church, where I was able to tell the story of our Order and invite the women of Jerusalem to join us. It was an answer to my prayers, and a day I will never forget to give thanks for.

Plaque outside Christ Church, Jerusalem

Praying at the Wailing Wall

As always, God's timing may not be ours. It was not until 2011 that the women of Christ Church were ready to institute the first chapter of Daughters of the King in the Middle East. After I was there in 2005, my dear friend and prayer partner, Andrea Evans, felt a call to live and work at Christ Church for 3 months in early 2006. Andrea was able to train 2 women, but we needed 3 to begin the chapter. One of the women she trained is on staff at the church. Another National Council member, Jennifer Mariano, was able to visit Christ Church in 2010 and meet with women who were interested in becoming Daughters. In the spring of 2011 the new rector, Rev. David Pileggi, agreed to form a DOK chapter. One of the ladies that Andrea had trained led the training for the others. They chose the name "Daughters of Jerusalem" for their chapter. I was blessed after I left office to go to Jerusalem to install the chapter on September 11, 2011. Pam Runyon, International Chair, accompanied me.

When I pinned the DOK cross on one of the women, she whispered in my ear, "I have believed in Jesus, the Messiah, for 20 years but this is the first cross I have ever had." (She is a Jewish believer come to faith in Jesus.) Tears of joy were in her eyes and mine. How wonderful to know that our ministry now is in the very city where Jesus, the Messiah, will return!

Pam Runyon, a world traveler, had never been to Israel until this trip. She and I loved every minute of our time there, and I felt then that the Lord might be preparing Pam for a greater role in our DOK ministry. It was at the next Triennial Retreat that Pam was elected National President. Praise God!

Christ Church, Jerusalem
Reverend David Pileggi and his wife, Carol with the banner for the new
Daughters of the King chapter

As I write this we have just learned that a Self-Denial Fund grant we sent to the Daughters of the Jerusalem this summer allowed them to send 3 missionaries to Turkey and Iraqi Kurdistan to aid the Christians fleeing from the violence. God is good!

Outside the Box

When my council had to decide where to hold our 2006 Triennial Retreat, we had several challenges. The General Convention that year was in early June, in Columbus, Ohio. June is not good for our membership, especially our teachers and Jr. Daughters. We wanted to be sure we had a venue and a date that would allow as many DOK and Jr. DOK as possible to attend.

Because our bylaws allow us flexibility is choosing our site (the bylaws say that we meet in the year of General Convention, not at the site), I asked our council to consider alternative sites and dates for our event. Several good suggestions were made, and after our Site Committee did their work, we decided that Orlando, Florida, the week of July 4 would be a good time and place for the meeting. It would give families an opportunity to come for a family vacation, and would be less expensive for air travel as well.

That was certainly "outside the box" thinking. Another change came when I decided to name an off-council Daughter to be the Triennial Chair. Since I had been Triennial Chair for 2003 in Minneapolis, I knew what the job entailed. My prayers on this decision were fierce and focused, and the Lord showed me that past National Council member, Deborah Tischler, would be my choice. She accepted the position, and did a marvelous job using her organizational and communication skills excellently. Deborah is also a dedicated prayer warrior, and I knew I could call on her for prayer assistance as needed.

The theme for this Triennial Retreat was "The Names of God," from Genesis to Revelation. The names that came to me immediately were these: Jehovah-Jireh, the Lord Our Provider; Jehovah-Rophe, the Lord Our Healer; Jehovah-Shalom, Jesus is Our Peace; El-Roi, the God Who Sees; and the Great I Am.

Our speakers were outstanding. Francis MacNutt taught Jehovah-Rophe, the Lord Our Healer; Dr. Theresa Newell taught El-Roi, the God Who Sees; and at our closing Eucharist, Bishop Frey's sermon was "The Great I Am."

Nancy McCann and the Glory Bound Singers were glorious, as always. Mrs. McCann even conducted a DOK Chorus at the closing banquet. However, her most beloved creation was "The Sister Act"; nuns who escorted in the Brotherhood of St. Andrew from their hotel nearby into our meeting room. The crowd of 600 plus exploded in applause and laughter as the nuns broke out into song -"My Guy." ("Nothing you can say can keep me away from My Guy.")

The GBS performing Sister Act

Nancy McCann and Stephanie in Sister Act

The Business Meeting took two days. I had determined to have a workshop on bylaw changes, and we did conduct that the night before the Triennial began. We had over 400 in attendance to discuss and debate the issues before us.

It was my responsibility to choose a Parliamentarian to assist us in the Business Meeting. I prayed about this and sought advice, and the Lord led me to choose Fr. Michael Gemignani, Diocese of Texas Chaplain. He not only is an Episcopal priest, but is a lawyer, and has served on several national boards as a Parliamentarian. His knowledge of Robert's Rules of Order is unmatched. Thank God he agreed to serve in this role. It proved a greater challenge than he or I could have imagined. It also proved to be an answer to prayer.

The morning of the second Business Meeting, before breakfast, I was surprised to open my hotel suite door to find 3 bishops standing there smiling. Bishop Frey, Bishop Bruce MacPherson, and Bishop William Skilton came in to reassure me that the delegates were in favor of equality of all members. Fr. Mike was already there with me when the bishops arrived. They prayed with me for courage, wisdom, and peace as the meetings had been quite volatile at times. It gave me great satisfaction to realize that these godly men had come to my aid.

The bishops were right. When the votes were counted – counted by our bishops – 80% of the delegates had voted to give voice and vote to our Anglican, Roman Catholic and Lutheran sisters. God is good!

Another highlight of the Triennial was conducting a joint Eucharist and rededication of vows with the Brotherhood of St. Andrews members. The

DOK began in 1885, and we took the formation of the Brotherhood in 1883 as our model. The service was inspiring for all of us in ministry.

We premiered the new DVD, "The Order of the Daughters of the King®, a Sisterhood" in Orlando. The council had been given an evangelism grant, and we used that grant money to create the DVD. Daughters across each province were asked to send their pictures, videos, and DVDs to us. Mr. Will VanNatta, Media Director of St. John the Divine in Houston, was our filmmaker. The "Sisterhood" DVD showed us around the world in ministry, and was especially touching when it highlighted the volunteer work done by Daughters during the Katrina Hurricane disaster.

Most thrilling to me personally was the participation of my father and mother, J.W. And Elwanda Burgess. They were so happy to be invited to the Triennial Retreat. Each day gave them more and more understanding of our Order. They loved International Night, and our dear friend, Dr. Deborah Ajakaiye, brought them special clothes made in Nigeria to wear for the occasion.

At Triennial with mom and dad

Me with Deborah Ajakaiye in Nigerian dress

The new National Council elected Joan Dalrymple to be our next National President. Joan is one of the original Glory Bound Singers. She and her husband, George, had moved to Colorado several years before this Triennial, but we still claimed her! When I was Diocese of Texas President, Joan agreed to be my Service Chair. She was splendid, and created a healing ministry called "The Balm of Gilead." After moving to Colorado, Joan was elected to National Council and served as National Secretary. Again, she did a very fine job.

When I pinned Margaret Franklin's pin on Joan during her installation I said, "Who knows but you have come to the kingdom, for such a time as this." Esther 4:14 That scripture proved to be prophetic during Joan's tenure as National President.

Others that were elected to that council had been and are very dear to me. Dr. Grace Sears had served Province 4 in many positions, and had been my Royal Cross Editor. The name "Grace" suits her perfectly. Grace was always kind and compassionate in all circumstances, and was very timely and on-point with the Royal Cross. At the next Triennial in 2009 Grace was elected as the next National President. It reminded me of when Jesus told the disciples in John 15, "Remember, I chose you; you did not choose me." Grace proved to be chosen for her time. It was Grace who gave me permission to represent her and the council in Jerusalem to install the Daughters of Jerusalem chapter on September 11, 2011. I am eternally grateful to her for this privilege.

If I wrote about all the women on council who are so outstanding, I would have an encyclopedia instead of a book. So I will not do that, but I will tell you of one more person that cannot be overlooked: Dr. Deborah Ajakaiye.

Dr. Deborah came to me when I was Diocese of Texas President at a Diocesan Assembly at St. Martin's Church in Houston. She stood in the crowd and asked me this, "What are you Daughters doing to EVANGELIZE Houston?" I stammered some lame answer, and then asked her to be my Evangelism Chair for Texas. She agreed without hesitation. We became fast friends and prayer partners.

Dr. Deborah is a geophysicist, born in Nigeria, educated in England. She is the foremost female scientist in her country, and has multiple awards to prove it. She has discovered oil fields around the world and in Nigeria. But her most commendable achievement comes from her compassionate and generous heart.

In 1994 Dr. Deborah was appalled by the devastation in Nigeria from the AIDS epidemic. She saw widows and orphans in every town and village. She decided to do something for them. She formed the CCWA – Christian Care for Widows, Orphans and the Aged. She opened 1 house with her own money, hired a manager and began to take in widows and orphans. Within a short time she had a second house and another and another. Today, 20 years later she has over 100 homes called centers in Nigeria, and 6 centers in Kenya. Between the widows, orphans and the aged, she has approximately 13,000 souls that she cares for each year.

Dr. Deborah not only feeds their bodies, but feeds their minds and their souls. She has set up classes to teach the women skills by which they can support themselves and their children. She has recently been given a land grant to enable her to build a school for these children and mothers. They also have access to Bible Study classes, and church meetings. Thousands have come to faith in Jesus by her witness.

Dr. Deborah served as International Chair during my tenure as President. She went wherever she was invited. Chapters were started in Ghana, Kenya, and Nigeria because of her work. Her most challenging invitation came to her by way of Cuba. An Anglican priest in Cuba asked for someone in the DOK to come and help him minister and start DOK chapters across his island. Dr. Deborah agreed to come, but that was not so easy. The USA does not have a travel agreement with Cuba. The Lord worked it out for Dr. Deborah to meet my friend and DOK, Laurel Wright, then of Pittsburgh, Pennsylvania. Laurel and her husband, the Rev. Mark Wright, had a mission agreement with Cuba. They had special permission to assist with mission trips each year to the island. However, Dr. Deborah and Laurel would have to go by way of Toronto, Canada – then on to Havana. Laurel and Dr. Deborah were able to plant 5 new DOK chapters in 2005 and those chapters are still active and growing today!

Deborah Ajakaiye and I have been close friends since we first met. She has stayed in my home, and I have stayed with her brother and sister-in-law in Paris. She has always wanted me to come to her home in Nigeria, but God has not made that happen, yet. Whenever I need a prayer partner, Deborah is there for me. The day before my hip replacement surgery, July 20, 2014, Deborah flew to be with me. It meant so much for me to have her by my side, praying for my healing. Her prayers are powerful, and I have had a fine recovery!

These are the highlights of Deborah Ajakaiye's term as International Chair:
- ❖ 2004, First chapter in Japan since WWII instituted
  - o First chapter in Germany instituted
- ❖ 2005, Daughters of the King assembled in the Virgin Islands
- ❖ 2006, 5 new chapters instituted in Cuba

More than 200 DOK chapters were instituted during my term! That includes 17 new Anglican chapters. Praise God! I thank God for the special women that I had the privilege to serve with on National Council for 9 years. I especially thank God for the 3 years I served as National President. It truly was the greatest honor of my life. Matthew 4:19 Jesus said, "Follow me, and be...."

Me dressed as Margaret Franklin with Laurie Ann Herman and
Deborah Ajakaiye

Me with Leslie Neville

Me with Marianne Smith and Marilyn Ligon

Ginny Zuppann and Martha Macdonald

Nancy McCann, Richard Foster, and me

Laurie Ann Herman and Helen Grace Wangusa

Joan Millard and Joan Dalrymple

Congratulations from Andrea Evans and Patsy Thomson

10 HAPPENING NOW -
REVIVAL IN MARSHALL, TEXAS

"In old age the righteous still produce fruit..." Psalm 92:14

In the fall of 2006 my husband and I made a move back to the place of my birth, Longview, Texas. My great-grandfather, James Madison Cecil Smith, had homesteaded his land in Gregg County starting in 1896. He came from Tennessee. He married my great-grandmother, Lela Sparks, and they had five daughters. My grandmother, Bertha, was one of the five and the most favorite person of my childhood. She died in 1992 but her memory is still strong in me today. I keep her picture on my dressing table. My boys called her "GG" since she was the great-grandmother.

Rich and I moved back to Longview because my parents were having health problems. It was good to be back in East Texas, in the pine forests where the trees turn gold and red in the fall. It was good to be able to help my parents and they helped us as well. We stayed in their home until we could purchase our own. My mother found the house we bought – just four blocks from their home.

Rich's stroke which afflicted him in 2004 left him disabled, but he was capable of staying home alone while I went back to work. His companion, a clever dachshund named Greta, kept him company during the day. Fortunately the Lord provided a good job for me just a few blocks from our new home, allowing us to have lunch together most days.

Mother and Dad were declining bit by bit in health during these years. By 2010 my mother was 85, and dad was 88. But I had a health surprise awaiting me. I developed Stage 1 breast cancer, and was successfully treated and healed by the grace of God. Only a lumpectomy and 6 weeks of radiation broke into my daily routine. No chemotherapy was needed. By September of 2010 I was declared "cancer free." The experience reminded me of how fragile we all are and how quickly life can change.

We loved our new home, built in 1957, but finding a church home was more challenging for us. We visited the Episcopal churches in town, but did not feel the Lord wanted us to join at that time. Then we met a delightful pastor of a Lutheran church, and he and Rich became fast friends. Pastor Darrell Howanitz had a heart for those with disabilities, and for that I am so grateful. His wife, Wanda, was such fun and we all became close friends. For two years we attended their church. When they left to take another call to a church in West Texas, we were searching again for where the Lord wanted us.

Then I remembered that the rector of Trinity Episcopal Church in Marshall, Texas, is the Rev. Dr. John Himes. Fr. John had been our Associate Rector in Houston at Ascension Church. Rich was excited to visit Fr. John's church. In the fall of 2011 we did visit, and knew right away that the Lord wanted us to settle there. It was 30 miles from our front door, but we did not care. We felt the Lord had brought us home.

Since "Revival" is my theme, I asked the Lord what HE wanted me to get involved in at my new church. The Daughters of the King chapter was not meeting regularly, and several of the women had asked me to help with renewal of interest in DOK. Eventually we decided that I would lead a Prayer Meeting one Sunday morning each month in our chapel before the worship service. With Fr. John's blessing we began to meet, and it was wonderful to see the response of the women who joined me.

On September 11, 2011, I was in Jerusalem installing the first chapter of Daughters of the King in the Middle East at Christ Church. The Daughters at Trinity in Marshall prayed me over to the Holy Land, and back. They were as excited as the Daughters of Jerusalem to join together with women in the very city where our Lord, Jesus, will return. We are truly a sisterhood.

Soon after we came to Trinity Church, I met and became friends with the Jr. Daughter Directress, Jennifer Howard. Jennifer reminded me of myself when I was her age. She is enthusiastic and visionary. She had a vision of how to draw young girls into the Jr. DOK ministry, and she wanted my advice. Her plans were outstanding, and she received Fr. John's approval to put them into action. Within months Jennifer had attracted young girls age 7-16 from all parts of our city. Within a few months Jennifer had the largest roster of girls in the USA. The girls came from every Christian denomination and ethnicity in the county. The girls pledged themselves to Prayer, Service and Evangelism. Jennifer asked several of the mothers to become her assistants, and they readily accepted. "Revival" was happening before our eyes. Many of the girls loved to sing, and soon we had the formation of a Jr. Daughter Choir, under the direction of Sr. DOK, Mary Price. The young choir premiered at our Christmas Eve family service in 2012, with twenty-four young voices singing beautiful carols. I was delighted to bring the Jr. DOK Choir to Camp Allen in September 2013 to sing for the Diocese of Texas Assembly. The Sr. Daughters were so blessed by these young ladies praising God in song.

Life changes were coming for us as we buried my beloved father in 2012 and my mother in 2013. They were in love their entire life together – all 66 years. Our son Drew was such a help to us during this time of my parents passing. Adam was not able to be with us as he was living and working in Ohio at the time.

Then my husband, Rich, had surgery in 2013, and I had surgery in 2014. Getting older is not for cowards! When our sons, Adam and Drew, realized our situation, they determined to help us. Fortunately, Adam was able to move to Longview in March of 2014. That was such a blessing for us all. Drew moved to Chicago, Illinois to explore the great north, so we were very pleased to have Adam close by.

Adam loves classical music and liturgical worship. He is a trained opera vocalist and soloist. Soon after he arrived at our home, he met with Fr. John and began singing in our choir. What a joy for him and for us! The choir members welcomed him, and Adam felt he was at home in our parish. That is a prayer answered.

Soon after Adam's arrival, he and Fr. John discussed what other ministries Adam might be interested in. Adam has known my work in the Daughters of the King, and he knew that the parallel ministry for men is The Brotherhood of St. Andrew. As soon as he discussed that with Fr. John, Adam spear-headed the work to REVIVE the Brotherhood chapter which had been active in our parish fifty years ago. Another prayer answered!

July 20, 2014 was the date of the installation of the re-organized chapter of the Brotherhood of St. Andrew, in which 9 men, including my son and my husband, took their vows to Pray, Serve and Study for the spread of Christ's kingdom. God is good, and I sense that HE is not finished with "Revival" at Trinity Church. The future holds promise!

Revival at Trinity that I have witnessed includes: Sr. Daughters of the King, Jr. Daughters of the King, the Brotherhood of St. Andrew, and our son Adam's renewed participation in church. How grateful I am to have seen God answer the question from Psalm 85:6, "Will you not revive us again, so that your people may rejoice in you?"

Our priest, Rev. Dr. John Himes, revived another tradition in September 2014, by creating a liturgy for us to use on Holy Cross Day. Fr. John proposed that we gather at the church and walk in procession behind the cross to specific sites in our city – praying for the city, the people, the needs, setting a hedge of protection around Marshall. Fr. John called this event the Prayer Walk. We invited others to join us and many came. This event was sponsored by the Jr. DOK, whose theme for the year of 2014 is: Keep It Holy.

When I examine my life of Prayer, Service, and Evangelism, it humbles me to realize that my husband has been the better evangelist. When Rich worked at a local newspaper in the 1990s, one of his editorial assistants, a young lady, came into his office and asked him to explain why he believed in God. Rich was shocked by the question, as he was a very quiet person in the workplace; but Rich kept a wooden paperweight on his desk that I had given him. The only word on engraved on the paperweight was "JESUS."

The young woman said she had heard Rich talking a lot about church, taking his sons to events there. Rich looked at her and said, "You had better let me call my wife – she is much better at this kind of talk than I am." The young woman said, "I do not know your wife – I know you."

Then Rich opened his bottom desk drawer, took out a Bible, and began to show her what he believed and why. Within two weeks he and the young lady had covered all that Rich could think to show her. Then he invited her to our church to hear our pastor. She came, and within weeks she was ready for her baptism. At her baptism the priest asked the sponsors (Rich and I), to name the person. She had never had a middle name, but Rich said to the priest, "Her name is Ingrid Christian." Rich gave her her middle name. She was delighted.

For four years during our time at Ascension in Houston, Rich joined Chuck Colson's Prison Fellowship. Each Thursday night he would drive out to the TC Jester Unit with three of his best friends and minister to men in prison. Rich loved this ministry. The last two years he participated, he mentored a young man named Julian who had been in prison since he was 20 years old. At the time Rich met him, he was 31 years old. Julian had come to faith in Jesus in prison. He told Rich that he would never be let out on parole, but Rich disagreed. Julian did not read and write very well. Rich, being a writer, determined to help him. Rich contacted his sister and his last employer, and got letters from them expressing their desire to help Julian have a home and job when released.

When the Parole Board met and reviewed Julian's file, they asked him who had put together his packet. He told them his friend Rich had done that. The Parole Board told Julian to thank his friend because they were granting Julian's parole, but would not have without that fine evidence. On Easter week Rich went to the prison and walked Julian to freedom. That is evangelism at its best. "If the Son sets you free; you shall be free indeed!" John 8:36

The only person I know for sure that came to faith because of my witness is my husband, Rich Lundgren. How do I know that? Because he told me so and my home fellowship group one night long ago at Ascension

Church. God is good!

As I am writing this chapter it is Advent, 2014. I love this season of expectation, this season of waiting for the Christ child. As I look over the last three years at Trinity Church, I marvel at what I have seen the Lord revive in our midst. I know in my heart that HE is not through with revival in our church, in our community, and most especially in each of us.

My other excitement this Advent is the release of our 20-Year CD for the Glory Bound Singers: "Come Holy Spirit." Actually this is our 23rd year together as a music ministry. It took a year to produce this CD, as we included many instruments that took extra recording time. I believe it is our best musical offering yet, and I am truly grateful to God, to Nancy McCann, and to Rock Romano for bringing this into creation. I pray that all who hear this music will be filled up with the Holy Spirit and experience REVIVAL in a real and personal way.

As we prepare this Advent for the birth of the Christ Child, I am reminded of the last prayer in Revelation:

"Come quickly, Lord Jesus!"
God bless you all now and forever,
    Sharon

Daughters of the King at Trinity, Marshall

Junior DOK choir singing at Camp Allen with Choir Directress, Mary Price

DOK Bonnie Strauss with Junior DOK Directress, Jennifer Howard

11 IN GRATITUDE TO MY CHAPLAINS

"I thank God upon every remembrance of you." Philippians 3:1

In July of 1991 our DOK Diocesan Chaplain was Suffragan Bishop, Rt. Rev. Anselmo Carral. Bishop Carral was originally from Cuba, and he was a beloved person in the Daughters of the King. I wrote him and asked his permission and blessing on our new music ministry, which we called The Glory Bound Singers. I asked if he would allow us to lead worship at DOK Diocesan Assemblies. He enthusiastically endorsed our new ministry, and was a constant supporter for many years and up until his death. Following Bishop Carral as chaplain was the Rev. Roland Timberlake, who accepted the invitation from Diocesan President Barbara Ward with enthusiasm.

When I was elected Diocese of Texas President in 1994, I was so pleased that the Rev. Roland Timberlake agreed to stay on during my tenure also. Roland and Alice Jean Timberlake are two of the most beloved people in the Diocese of Texas. Roland served for many years as rector of St. Luke's on the Lake Episcopal Church in Austin, Texas. He retired from that church, and now serves as rector emeritus there.

Alice Jean has been a beloved Bible teacher and retreat leader for women all across our diocese and our state. She is also beloved by the Daughters of the King, and I call her our unofficial "godmother."

When I was elected to be the Province 7 President in 1997, again I was honored that Roland agreed to serve as our provincial chaplain during my tenure. It was a time of growth for our province, and his strong leadership and focus always helped me see what the next goal should be in the Lord's greater plan. His strong stand for Biblical teaching always gave me a sense of well-being as I needed his advice on situations that could be quite sensitive. (Sadly I must report that Roland Timberlake died suddenly on

January 6, 2015 – Epiphany – after a fall at his home. Over 700 attended his funeral. We will miss him, but know we shall all see him again in Glory!)

The next chaplain to whom I am indebted is the Rev. Michael Gimignani, who served as Diocese of Texas Chaplain after Chaplain Timberlake, and still serves as Province 7 Chaplain as of this writing. Because the Glory Bound Singers lead worship at all Diocese of Texas assemblies, Fr. Mike long ago became a favorite of mine. He is also a gifted songwriter, and we have sung many of his songs of praise or meditation. However, Fr. Mike's greatest service to me was his service as Parliamentarian for the Business Meeting at the Orlando Triennial in 2006. God bless him!

The next chaplain was of course Rt. Rev. William Frey, National Chaplain during my presidential tenure 2003-2006. In my chapter entitled "Presidential Memories," you will read of Bishop Frey's great contribution to our Order and to my spiritual well-being. His service and care of the Daughters of the King is truly a priceless gift of love.

Scripture says, "The first shall be last; the last shall be first." It is good for me to remind us that our first chaplains as Daughters are our priests of the local parishes we are members of. In my lifetime Rev. Joseph DiRaddo, of Epiphany in Houston, Rev. Dr. Albert S. Lawrence, of Ascension in Houston, and today Rev. Dr. John Himes of Trinity in Marshall are the outstanding chaplains that have guided me throughout my life as a Daughter of the King. Rev. Dr. Al Lawrence has also been my editor for this book! He is a published writer, and has helped me tremendously in my journey through this last year. Thank you, Al!

Let us remember to lift up our chaplains in prayer for their protection, strength, discernment of God's truth, and continued ministry to us all. Let us also remember to offer our acts of service to our chaplains whenever they need our assistance. Charity really should begin at home - in our home parishes!

Bishop Carral with Adam, 1990

Fr. Joe DiRaddo, Nancy McCann, and Fr. Mike Gemignani

Fr. John Himes and my grandson, Jacob

Rev. Roland Timberlake

11 EPILOGUE – EASTER 2015

"....a time to break down, and a time to build up; a time to weep, and a time to laugh...." Ecclesiastes - Chapter 3

In my last chapter I was writing during Advent 2014. Many changes have occurred in my life since then. My husband's health began to break down during Lent. On March 9 when I came home from work at 5:00PM, Rich was lying face down on the kitchen floor – not moving. I said a quick prayer and called his name. He answered me saying he was OK, but he could not get up. He was not OK. I called 911 and we eventually transported him to the hospital.

Over the course of the next week Rich suffered several strokes, which were debilitating. A week after he was stabilized, we transferred him to a nursing home in Marshall, TX, just 5 blocks from our son, Adam.

Easter Sunday Rich was able to come to lunch with our family in a wheelchair. He cannot walk yet, and we hope and pray that the medications and physical therapy will allow him to eventually walk with a walker. Rich enjoyed being with the family, and ate a bit of his favorite foods, even though he cannot really feed himself yet. He laughed when people told funny stories, but did not converse except to say "yes" or "no". His life has changed and so has mine.

On March 19 we celebrated our 39th wedding anniversary, in the nursing home. To everything there is a time and a season.

The good news is that our God is an awesome God. He is EL-ROI, The God Who Sees. God knew that this downturn in health was coming for Rich and God allowed Rich two wonderful events before this health crisis.

In early February I took Rich to the Longview News-Journal to be interviewed by a longtime co-worker of Rich's, Glenn Evans. Glenn interviewed Rich about his historic interview he had in 1985 with President Ronald Reagan. Glenn's interview of Rich appeared on the front page of the LNJ on President's Day, February 16, 2015. It was grand, and Rich loved telling the story and seeing it recounted by Glenn in the newspaper. Then on March 5 Rich and I took Glenn out to supper as a "thank you" for his work on the story. Rich had a marvelous time, and it was like a reunion. Sitting across the restaurant was another of Rich's newspaper friends from long ago, and she came over to visit as well. Her name is Ingrid, and you may remember her from another chapter about her coming to faith in the workplace, partly through Rich's witness.

God is good!

The next day is when Rich started his physical downturn.

El-Roi, The God Who Sees, saw to it that Rich had 2 wonderful months of joy before he suffered in this new physical battle. God also sees what the future holds for Rich and for me as we live our lives, separately, but together.

My book was to be in print in March, however, these things and others prevented the proof copy from being finished. Perhaps it was because the Lord wanted me to write this Easter chapter!

No matter what the future brings, I hope to stand firm on Romans 8:38:

"I am convinced that neither death, nor life, nor angels, nor rulers, nor things present, nor things to come, nor powers, nor height, nor depth, nor anything else in all creation, will be able to separate us from the love of God in Christ Jesus, our Lord."

June 4, 2015 - Rich died

Oct. 26, 2015 - Nancy died

I still stand on

Romans 8:38 →

ABOUT THE AUTHOR

Sharon Lundgren was born and raised in Texas. Most of her life was spent in Houston with her husband, Rich Lundgren. Rich was a writer/editor for the Houston Post newspaper, and Sharon worked part-time for various medical/dental facilities.

In 2006, Sharon moved to Longview with her husband, who had become disabled by a stroke. She went to work full-time for a local dentist as office manager, and continues in that position today. She and her husband have two grown sons, one grandson, and one granddaughter.

Sharon has been a Daughter of the King for more than half her life. The Daughters of the King religious order was created in 1885 by Episcopalian women dedicated to serving the church through Prayer, Service, and Evangelism. Today the DOK membership includes Anglican, Roman Catholic, and Lutheran women around the world.

She loves her work in ministry as a Daughter, and has served in many local and national positions, including National President of The Order of the Daughters of the King® from 2003-2006.

The Lundgrens, Christmas 2014

Made in the USA
San Bernardino, CA
16 March 2017